Cornerstones of Freedom

The Panama Canal

BARBARA GAINES WINKELMAN

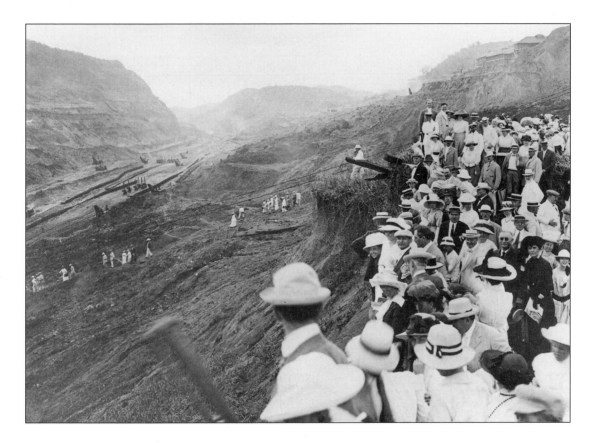

CHILDREN'S PRESS®
A Division of Grolier Publishing
New York • London • Hong Kong • Sydney
Danbury, Connecticut

Visit Children's Press on the Internet at:
http://publishing.grolier.com

Library of Congress Cataloging-in-Publication Data

Winkelman, Barbara Gaines, 1961–
    The Panama Canal / Barbara Gaines Winkelman.
        p. cm.—(Cornerstones of freedom)
    Includes index.
    Summary: Relates the history of how the Panama Canal was built and
studies the economic and political consequences of its construction.
    ISBN: 0-516-21142-0 (lib. bdg.)   0-516-26460-5 (pbk.)
    1. Panama Canal (Panama)—History—Juvenile literature. [1. Panama Canal
(Panama)—History.] I. Title. II. Series.
F1569.C2W56   1999
972.87'5—dc21

                                                    98–3493
                                                       CIP
                                                       AC

It was December 2, 1823, in Washington, D.C. Members of the United States Congress were hushed and sitting on the edge of their seats. They were about to listen to the annual address of the nation's fifth president, James Monroe. Congress had heard that this day's speech would be important to the young United States. After much anticipation, the president delivered his now-famous Monroe Doctrine.

James Monroe served as president of the United States from 1817 to 1825.

In his speech, President Monroe gave a strong message to the powerful countries of Europe: If you continue to colonize, we will stop you; you have abused your colonies long enough. In other words, the United States promised to help fight the oppression that its people had experienced when the land was controlled by Great Britain, Spain, France, and other European powers.

Did President Monroe know that in the coming years the meaning of his words would be changed again and again? His speech resulted in a dilemma, or problem. Congress and others wondered how the young United States would combine its need for growth with the belief that each country should be free to rule itself. It was not an easy dilemma to solve, especially when it came to a vital bridge of land that connected east to west—the isthmus of Panama. (An isthmus is a narrow strip of land with water on each side.)

Panama is a country in Central America, the narrow, southern portion of land that connects the continents of North and South America. Central America lies between the Pacific Ocean and the Caribbean Sea.

The Panama Canal is 51 miles (80 kilometers) long. It is located between Panama City on the Pacific coast to Colón on the coast of the Caribbean Sea. (The Caribbean Sea leads into the Atlantic Ocean.) Construction of this canal was not only a major engineering accomplishment, but it also was a political and economic victory for the United States.

The Panama Canal enabled merchants and navies to sail from the Atlantic Ocean to the Pacific without making the long, dangerous, and expensive 13,000-mile (21,000-km) trip around the tip of South America. As a result, the canal yielded great economic and political power. The country that controlled it was allowed to charge crossing fees to the ships, as well as shut down the canal to enemies. To gain these advantages, powerful countries kept an interest in building a canal in Panama—a land full of dense forests, tropical jungles, vast mountains, and harsh weather.

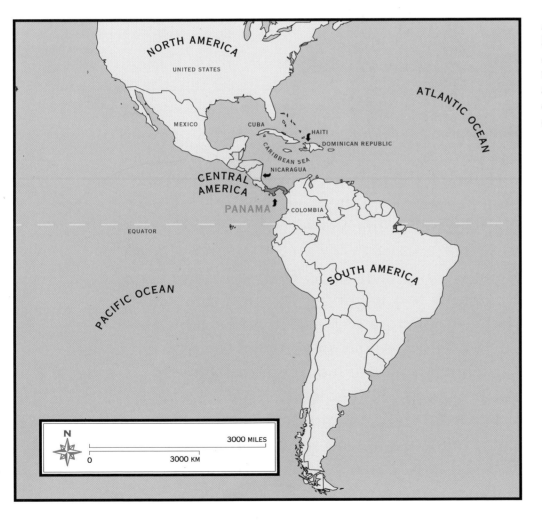

Panama's location between North and South America made it an ideal site for the construction of a canal.

Vasco Núñez de Balboa

The existence of an isthmus between the two great seas was discovered by the Spanish explorer Vasco Núñez de Balboa. In 1510, Balboa was living on the Spanish island in the Caribbean Sea that is now made up of the countries of Haiti and the Dominican Republic. After nine years there, Balboa found himself in debt. He escaped from his money problems by hiding on a Spanish ship bound for Central America.

Balboa led a mutiny, or revolt, against the ship's captain, and became a great leader. The ship docked in the waters surrounding what is now the coast of Colombia. But the Indians there were too fierce. So Balboa led the Spaniards to a friendlier location that he had visited on an expedition about ten years earlier. The Spanish established their own settlement, and the local Indians showed them where to find gold.

The local Indians told Balboa that there was a great body of water at the other end of the land. Dressed in full armor, Balboa and his men set out in search of this sea. Their progress was slow, as they cut their way through dense jungle in extreme heat. Many men got sick from dysentery, an infection that causes severe diarrhea. Others were slowed by painful cuts from the underbrush. Throughout the journey, Balboa befriended the local Indians so that he and his men could pass through their land.

Balboa and his men encountered many hardships on their journey through the jungle.

Finally, on September 25, 1513, Balboa became the first European to see the eastern shore of the Pacific Ocean. After another four days spent reaching the water, Balboa declared the "Great South Sea" a Spanish territory.

As his men bowed in prayers of thanksgiving, Balboa stood in the Pacific Ocean and claimed it as a Spanish possession on September 29, 1513.

The Spanish began to build El Camino Real, or The Royal Road, across Panama to connect the two great bodies of water. The road was completed in about 1522.

During the next three hundred years, the Spanish stronghold on and around The Royal Road was unsteady, as buccaneers (robbers) from France, Holland, and Great Britain would attack the Spanish and steal their gold. But the Spanish persevered and dreamed about building a canal that connected the two seas at Panama.

The Spanish cut through dense forest similar to this as they built The Royal Road.

Spain came close to beginning construction of a canal in 1814, when the king ordered a canal to be built. However, four years later, in 1818, Colombia became the first of several Spanish territories to revolt against Spain. As a result, Spain no longer controlled the area. On November 10, 1821, Panama declared its independence from Spain. But Panama quickly became part of Colombia because the Panamanians did not have enough money or military force to start their own nation.

Spain was not the only country that dreamed of an interoceanic canal. And Panama was not the only place where other countries were thinking of building a canal. Explorers also suggested Nicaragua or Mexico. But no country yet had the technology or the money to accomplish such a project.

The United States had also been interested in building the canal, but it did not have the funds or power until the early 1900s. But, to protect any interests it could have in the canal, the United States negotiated a treaty with Colombia in 1846. Called the Bidlack Treaty, this agreement gave the U.S. government free passage across Panama using any type of transportation—including transportation that had not yet been built. Therefore, the United States acquired free passage across any canal that might be built after the treaty was signed.

In return, the United States guaranteed that the isthmus would be neutral. This meant that if a conflict arose in Panama, the United States would help to stop it by sending soldiers, weapons, or money. The United States also guaranteed that Panama would always be a part of Colombia.

The United States's interest in a Panamanian canal increased in 1848, when gold was discovered in California. Thousands of people headed west to dig fortunes for themselves. People from the eastern United States found it easiest to sail south to Panama, cross the isthmus on the old Royal Road, and then take a ship north to California. Soon, so many people were traveling that route between 1850 and 1855 that a railroad was built across Panama.

Although the railroad made travel through Panama easier, its construction was long and difficult.

During the railroad's construction, the U.S. government caught a glimpse of how difficult it would be to build a canal in Panama. In the worst year, 1852, forty-eight of fifty American workers died while building the railroad. A total of six thousand workers died in Panama. The technicians and workers could not overcome the horrors of the Panamanian isthmus. They battled the sickness from malaria, yellow fever, dysentery, cholera, and smallpox, the harshness of the wild jungle that had to be cut back, the reptiles and wild animals, and the hills that had to be climbed. Even worse, the weather was another barrier. Not only was it extremely hot, but there was also an eight-month rainy season. The constant rain caused massive mudslides in the mountains and hills of central Panama.

It took five years to complete a single-track railroad of only 50 miles (80 km). The railroad was successful until 1869 when the Transcontinental Railroad was built across the United States, allowing even quicker access to the West.

In Panama, workers were constantly exposed to yellow fever, malaria, and other illnesses.

The United States was unhappy when two European powers began to build a canal that connected the Atlantic and Pacific Oceans. First, Great Britain decided to build a canal in Nicaragua. The United States insisted that Great Britain was violating the Monroe Doctrine, which warned against European invasion of any former European colony. Nicaragua was a former Spanish colony, and Great Britain could not invade it by building a canal. The United States believed that it could fix this violation by joining Great Britain in building and controlling a canal. In 1850, the United States and Great Britain signed the Clayton-Bulwer Treaty, which allowed for the two countries to build a canal in either Nicaragua or Panama.

About thirty years later, France decided to build a canal across Panama. But the French government did not have enough money to complete the project. In 1879, the government negotiated with a French company to raise funds for building the canal. The government would give the company a share of the fees collected from shippers who used the canal. The president of this French company was Ferdinand de Lesseps. De Lesseps led the construction of Egypt's Suez Canal, which was completed in 1869.

Before construction of a Panamanian canal could begin, de Lesseps had to decide which

Ferdinand de Lesseps

type of canal to build: either a sea-level canal or a lock canal. A sea-level canal is built at the same distance above sea level at every point. A lock canal is used when the canal is not at the same sea level throughout. The ships in a lock canal are raised and lowered onto different canal heights by the filling and emptying of giant containers called locks. As the ship floats into a lock, the lock is filled with water. The flow of the water lifts the ship up to a higher level. The lock is drained when the ship passes through to a lower sea level.

A lock canal consists of water-filled chambers, or locks, that raise and lower ships from one lock to another. These locks were built in pairs to allow ships traveling in different directions to pass through at the same time.

15

The canal was to be constructed through one of Panama's highest hills, Culebra Cut, which was 300 feet (91 meters) high. If a sea-level canal was built, it would be almost impossible to dig through such a high hill. (The proper equipment did not exist.) Therefore, the engineers recommended that they build a lock canal so that ships could be lifted over the hill and then lowered back down again on the other side. But de Lesseps insisted that he had successfully built a sea-level canal at the Suez, and the same should be used for Panama.

Engineers and surveyors carefully studied the land and jungle to develop a plan for the canal.

The French began digging a sea-level canal in 1881. But they faced the same deadly obstacles that had plagued the workers building the Panamanian railroad: extreme heat, heavy rainfall, and mudslides. Sickness and disease were common among the workers. About sixteen thousand workers died from yellow fever and malaria.

Other problems plagued de Lessep's company, including corruption and mismanagement. Eventually the company went bankrupt. Construction of the canal ended in 1889, eight years after it began. However, the company did complete a large portion of the canal.

De Lessep's workers completed only a portion of the canal before construction ended as a result of illness, disease, harsh weather, and bankruptcy.

The next attempt to build a canal was the final, successful effort by the United States. In 1898, the Spanish-American War made the construction of a canal important to the safety of the United States. The war was fought in two Spanish territories on both sides of the United States—Cuba in the Caribbean Sea and the Philippines in the Pacific Ocean.

The United States did not have quick access to either Cuba or the Philippines because of their distant locations. Another problem developed during the fighting: The United States had to send its battleship, *Oregon,* to Cuba. But the ship was docked in San Francisco, California. To reach Cuba, the ship had to race all the way around the southern tip of South America—a journey of 13,000 miles (21,000 km). It would have been a lot quicker and less expensive if the ship could have traveled through an interoceanic canal.

The Spanish-American War lasted just four months, but the United States government realized that it was time to build the canal. The government decided to construct the canal in Panama, instead of Nicaragua.

Before the United States could begin building the canal, however, it had to overcome some hurdles. In 1901, the United States bought the partial canal that had been built by de Lessep's company, as well as all of the company's equipment. Next, the United States eliminated

Much of the abandoned equipment used by the French was bought by the United States in 1901.

the Clayton-Bulwer Treaty of 1850 that required the United States to build the canal with Great Britain. The U.S. government asserted that the treaty violated the Monroe Doctrine because it would force the United States to share control of the canal with a European Power.

Great Britain unexpectedly agreed to cancel the treaty. As a result, the United States and Great Britain reached an agreement that the United States would act alone in Panama.

Theodore Roosevelt (top) and John Hay (above) led the United States's effort to gain permission to build the Panama Canal.

The last obstacle was gaining Colombia's permission to build a canal in Panama. (Panama was still a part of Colombia.) The United States, under President Theodore Roosevelt and Secretary of State John Hay, asked Colombia for permission to dig the canal. The Colombian leaders agreed. But the Colombian Congress would not ratify, or approve, the agreement because the Congress wanted more money from the United States than the amount stated in the agreement. President Roosevelt was angry, but determined to build the canal.

Meanwhile, Panamanians grew increasingly unhappy under Colombia's control. They had rebelled five times between 1846 and 1900. In 1903, when the Panamanians heard that Colombia refused to allow the United States to build a canal, they planned another revolt.

This time, the Panamanians were successful because President Roosevelt supported their revolt. Roosevelt sent ten U.S. warships to Panama City, and the gunboat *Nashville* to Colón. The *Nashville* arrived in time to prevent the Colombian troops from traveling across the Panamanian isthmus.

Roosevelt also sent a large military force to Panama. Colombia was powerless against it. Three days later, the Panamanian leaders declared Panama's independence from Colombia.

Shortly after, the Hay-Bunau-Varilla Treaty gave the United States control of an area called the Panama Canal Zone. The Canal Zone stretched for 5 miles (8 km) on each side of the canal. The United States was also given the authority to stop any revolution or political unrest in Panama City or Colón. It also could claim any land outside the Canal Zone, if it was considered necessary for the defense of the canal. Finally, the United States guaranteed Panama's independence, and would enter any conflict that threatened the new republic. Under the treaty, the United States was allowed to enter Panama at any time without Panama's permission. All of these actions were allowed forever. Many people believed that Panama had actually become a territory of the United States.

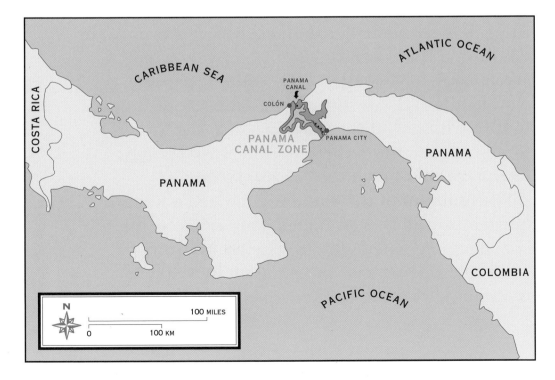

The Panama Canal Zone was a total of 10 miles (16 km) wide and 40 miles (64 km) long.

President Roosevelt on a steam shovel during a 1906 visit to a construction site at the canal

Although the Panamanians strongly disapproved of the treaty, they were excited about the canal. They expected a boost in their economy from the jobs that would be created by the presence of the United States. But most of the workers on the Panama Canal were not Panamanian. They were citizens of Jamaica, the United States, and Europe.

The U.S. government gave two reasons for not hiring Panamanians. First, that Panamanians were small people and their size would prevent them from doing the heavy lifting required by canal work. Second, the United States wanted the workers to speak English because leaders believed that workers who could not communicate effectively would slow down construction. The United States claimed its right to control the Canal Zone, and to hire whomever it wanted because the United States needed to protect the time, money, and resources that had already been spent.

The building of the canal was indeed a huge burden for the United States. Preparations for construction lasted almost four years, from 1903–07. During that time, the United States built homes for the workers, post offices,

courthouses, police and fire departments, and other government offices. Another rail line was added to the Panamanian railroad to cart away the millions of tons of dirt that were excavated.

An important part of the preparation involved medicine. If the project was to be successful, yellow fever and malaria had to be eliminated. Fortunately, in the late 1800s, scientists discovered that a certain type of mosquito spread these diseases. By 1901, Colonel William C. Gorgas, the U.S. Army's chief sanitation officer, had almost

completely wiped out the diseases in Cuba by killing the mosquitoes and destroying their nesting grounds. He successfully applied the same method to eliminate the mosquitoes in Panama, and the diseases no longer posed a threat to the workers.

George Goethals, builder of the Panama Canal

Meanwhile, the United States had formed the Panama Canal Commission to oversee construction. After the first two chief engineers quit, President Roosevelt appointed George Goethals as head of the commission and chief engineer. Goethals provided the leadership needed to get the work done. He divided the workers into three crews: one starting from Panama City and heading east, the second starting from Colón and heading west, and the third starting in the middle and slicing through the treacherous Culebra Cut, which was renamed the Gaillard Cut in 1915. When these three crews met, the work would be done.

It took about seven years, from 1907–13, to build the canal. During that time, the workers overcame the harsh land and weather of Panama, making the building of the canal a tremendous feat. Again the workers faced harsh weather: humidity, blazing sunshine, floods, and landslides from the

The noise made by the huge machinery was so loud that workers often could not hear each other speak.

heavy rain. The workers were subjected to the deafening roar of the loud machinery. Sometimes the hills they were digging into gave way, resulting in massive landslides that ruined weeks of work.

The three crews finally met each other in May 1913. The work continued, and on August 15, 1914, the S.S. *Ancon* became the first ship to complete the trip through the canal. The commission adopted the motto: "The Land Divided, The World United."

In the canal's first year of operation, five million tons of cargo passed through it. By the 1960s, almost 170 million tons passed through each year. In 1996, 15,187 ships sailed through the canal, carrying 198 million tons of cargo.

Visitors watch as the last dam is exploded to celebrate the opening of the Panama Canal on October 10, 1913.

While the world passed through Panama, the country did not enjoy its status as a "land divided." The Canal Zone had literally split Panama in two. Controlled by the United States, the Zone had its own language (English), its own set of laws, a post office system, and a hospital system. Only U.S. flags were flown in the Canal Zone. Panamanians could not travel from one side of the country to the other until the early 1960s, when the United States built a bridge on the Pacific Ocean side of the canal. Discrimination also existed in the Zone. For example, Panamanians were paid less than U.S. citizens for the same jobs.

Little by little, Panama gained more control of the Canal Zone. In 1936, the Hull Alfaro Treaty ended the United States's guarantee of Panamanian independence, as well as its right to intervene in Panamanian conflicts. In 1955, another treaty granted equal pay and working conditions for Panamanians who worked in the Zone. In 1962, leaders of Panama and the United States agreed that Panamanian flags could fly beside American flags.

The flags of Panama (left) and the United States (right) fly in front of the U.S. Naval Station in Panama.

Finally, in 1977, the Panamanians got what they wanted. President Jimmy Carter signed two treaties that provided for a gradual, twenty-year transfer of control of the canal from the United States to Panama. These treaties, called the Carter-Torrijos Treaties, called for the Canal Zone to dissolve on October 1, 1979, and for the canal to remain permanently neutral. The Panamanian government would take complete control of the canal at noon on December 31, 1999.

U.S. president Jimmy Carter (seated, left) and Panamanian leader General Omar Torrijos (seated, right) signed one of the Carter-Torrijos Treaties on September 7, 1977.

Under the treaties, the Panama Canal Commission will run the canal until the last day of 1999. This commission is part of the United States government and is composed of both Panamanians and U.S. citizens. In 1990, a Panamanian led the commission, which was composed mostly of Panamanians. This was the first time in U.S. history that a United States government agency was headed by a non-U.S. citizen.

During the twenty-year transfer of ownership of the canal, discrimination against the Panamanians has decreased dramatically. By October 1995, most of the key jobs in the canal were filled by Panamanians. In addition, the 1977 treaties provided that U.S. citizens working in Panama are subject to Panamanian law.

Why did the United States agree to give Panama control of the canal? The reason may be that the military value of the canal has decreased because the United States now fights mainly from the air with modern bomber planes and missiles. At the time of the treaties, the canal had been losing money since the early 1970s, when merchant ships became bigger. The canal was too small for these giant ships. To make the canal big enough to handle them, it would have had to be rebuilt into a sea-level canal. Once again, this would have required a tremendous amount of resources.

Did the United States give up the canal that it worked so hard to build because it wanted to right its wrongs against Panama? Or did the United States simply give up an old gem that had lost its value? Perhaps both. But it may be more important that, in 1999, Panama—for the first time in its history—will be one nation. It will no longer be divided or controlled by another country. For the first time since the 1500s, Panamanians will control their entire nation.

As this ship prepares to enter the locks of the canal, the nation of Panama prepares for a new chapter in its history.

GLOSSARY

bankrupt – out of money, or financially ruined

colonize – to establish a new territory that has been settled by people from another country and is controlled by that country

discrimination – prejudice or unjust behavior to others based on differences in age, gender, race, or other factors

economy – the way a country runs its industry, trade, and finance

excavate – to dig in the earth

Workers used huge machines to excavate the land.

interoceanic – between two oceans

intervene – to become involved in a situation in order to change what is happening

merchant – someone who sells goods for profit

motto – short sentence that is meant to state what someone believes in or stands for

navy – all of a country's warships, aircraft, weapons, land bases, and personnel

oppression – treatment of others in a cruel, unjust, and harsh way

republic – form of government in which the people have the power to elect representatives who manage the government

Colonel Gorgas was the U.S. Army's chief sanitation officer.

sanitation officer – military person in charge of preventing disease by promoting clean conditions in which to live and work

sea level – the average level of the surface of the ocean

territory – part of the United States that is not admitted as a state

tropical – anything that refers to the tropics, the extremely hot area of Earth near the equator

TIMELINE

Panama declares independence from Spain **1821**
Monroe Doctrine **1823**

Bidlack Treaty **1846**
Gold discovered in California **1848**
Clayton-Bulwer Treaty **1850**

1855 Railroad built across Panama

1881

1889

1898 Spanish-American War

1901

De Lessep's company begins constructing canal

United States buys de Lessep's canal; Clayton-Bulwer Treaty cancelled

1903 Panama gains independence from Colombia; Hay-Bunau-Varilla Treaty

1907
Panama Canal constructed
1913

1914 Panama Canal opens

1936 Hull Alfaro Treaty

1955 Treaty grants workers equal pay

1962

Carter-Torrijos Treaties **1977**
Canal Zone dissolved **1979**

Panama takes control of canal and Canal Zone **1999**

Panamanian flags allowed in Canal Zone

INDEX (*Boldface page numbers indicate illustrations.*)

PHOTO CREDITS

Photographs ©: Cameramann International, Ltd.: 26, 31 bottom; Corbis-Bettmann: 24 top (George Rinhart), 23 top (Underwood & Underwood), cover, 1, 8, 14, 23 bottom, 25, 27, 30 bottom; North Wind Picture Archives: 11, 12, 13, 16, 17, 20 top, 31 top, 31 center; Stock Montage, Inc.: 3, 6, 7, 15, 19, 20 bottom, 22, 24 bottom, 30 top; Tony Stone Images: 2, 29 (Will and Deni McIntyre), 9 (Art Wolfe); maps: TJS Design, Inc.

ABOUT THE AUTHOR

Barbara Gaines Winkelman attended the University of Pennsylvania, where she received a bachelor's degree in English. She went on to law school at the Benjamin Cardozo School of Law in New York.

Ms. Winkelman has written several children's books, including a first reader series featuring Winnie the Pooh, *Countdown to Extinction*, a chapter book for six to eight year olds, and *Flying Squirrel of Acorn Place*. She currently writes full time and lives in Westport, Connecticut, with her husband Bill, son A.J., and daughter Hannah.